Going Broke Staying Sane

Facing Adversity and Starting Again

RICHARD SHRAPNEL

Published in 2021 by Wilkinson Publishing Pty Ltd
ACN 006 042 173
PO Box 24135, Melbourne, VIC 3001, Australia
Ph: +61 3 9654 5446
enquiries@wilkinsonpublishing.com.au
www.wilkinsonpublishing.com.au

[f] WilkinsonPublishing

[◎] wilkinsonpublishinghouse

[🐦] WPBooks

Cover and book design by Tango Media
Printed and bound in Australia by Griffin Press, a part of Ovato

ISBN: 9781925927726
A catalogue record for this book is available from the National Library of Australia.

My Copy

My Name
....

Started
....

Completed
....

If found, please contact me via the details below:

T:
....

E:
....

This simple guide is for those who are confronted with the loss of their business. I hope it will support you to journey forward through this adversity and emerge more or less intact. There will be scars, that is the nature of adversity, but finding that solid footing again, scars and all, is what your goal should be.

Richard Shrapnel.

Contents

An Active Resource

Here are some thoughts and ideas as to how to gain the most out of reading this guide.

It's Not Just A Book

This is not just a book—it's a guide, a workbook, and an active resource.

It has been conceived not just to read but to:

▶ Write all over.

▶ Highlight everything that rings true.

▶ Make reminders.

▶ Capture thoughts.

▶ Initiate actions.

▶ Ask questions.

▶ Doodle on as much as you want.

▶ Just imagine what may be possible.

▶ Use in any way that stimulates your thinking.

Its aim is to provide you with a framework for thought and to guide thinking, analysis, argument, understanding, and, most importantly, action.

It can be applied anywhere, anytime, and to each and every individual and unique business.

It should become a resource and place for your thoughts, to which you will continually return as a critical reference.

The Power of the Pencil

This guide is designed for you to write all over it. There is a forgotten power in using a pencil on paper that this guide will allow you to recapture.

Unlocking your deep knowledge and experiences:

Holding a pencil in your hand and connecting it with paper as you read can be the key to unlocking potential within that you did not know still existed.

We actually don't consciously know most of what is held in our mind. There are deep knowledge and experiences that we have stored over our years of life that have been forgotten. They are locked away in the recesses of our mind and covered by the stress and tensions of modern life and business.

However, by using your hands to explore questions and opportunities and to explore the world, you can begin to open these recesses and to release wisdom you had all but forgotten. Using your hands is a very primal way through which your brain constructs its own knowledge of the world. Picking things up, holding them, and wondering what they are all about is a profoundly human thing to do.

Using your hands can allow you to unleash creative energies, modes of thought, and ways of seeing things that you may have forgotten were within. And in times of adversity you should seek to tap into these reserves.

Pick up your pencil, roll it between your fingers, chew on its end, stick it behind your ear as you consider what is explored in this guide, write out your answers and thoughts. This tactile connection between hand and mind and thoughts will yield a powerful response.

Lifting the ceiling on your success:
Crafting and describing the 'new you/new business' in writing—by your own hand—as you work your way through this guide will materially strengthen the possibility of it becoming real.

The image you hold of yourself and your business creates the ceiling to how successful you can be. It's a subconscious barrier that you cannot break—but you can rewrite it. As you strive to achieve in life, your subconscious is constantly asking, 'Is this me? Is this what I do? Am I this person?' If the answer is 'yes', your actions are reinforced and all is good. But if the answer is 'no' then your inbuilt safety switch kicks in, your subconscious says, 'No, I am not this successful, I should fail', and therefore you do.

As you work through this guide you should begin to reimagine what your life and business could be. As you read each paragraph, as you answer each question that comes to mind, you should begin to also draw a new picture of who you and your business are.

You want to develop a new image of what is possible and the goals you are going to achieve. To make this new image real you will need to transfer it from your conscious mind to your subconscious mind. You will want to imprint this new image in your subconscious and overwrite the old image that has been holding you back. It will become the new basis of who you are.

You will craft and describe this new image, what you are going to do and change to bring it about, the compelling reasons for why it will happen, and your plan to achieve it. And the most effective way of imprinting this new image and commitment in your subconscious is by writing it out by hand, time and time again.

Taking your pencil in your hand and reimaging who you are and what your business is imprints this image on your subconscious. The more often you do it, the stronger that image will become.

Craft this new image on page 96 to reinforce your strength as you journey forward through the current challenges.

Preface

Yesterday

It's just after midnight on 1 January 2020, a new year and a new decade have just shone through. The possibilities and opportunities for great things to happen are evident and real. Not just the drawing of a line on the close of another year but also the close of a decade. Imagine what can be achieved over this new decade, the excitement is real.

Today

And then the world sneezes and everyone, *everyone*, is impacted. The unknown has become ever-present, and the fear throughout our communities is palpable. Illness and death are spreading, jobs are being lost, and businesses are failing—the uncertainty of what may lay ahead over the days and weeks to come seems to have no limit.

Tomorrow

Many businesses will be lost, many will also evolve, and some will prosper, but the lives of the owners and employees of all businesses will be impacted. And a future will emerge no matter how dim the light at the end of that tunnel may presently seem for you and your business.

That future, *your* future, will be set by how you confront the challenges and losses that may cross your path and will certainly cross the paths of many whom you know.

The journey you decide for yourself now will set the cornerstone for your future and who you are and become as a person and a leader.

There is no place for spectators. And as for the opportunists, those who wish to profiteer and take advantage of those who may be weakened, well, let us not support them in their acts of self interest.

No spectators, you are either fighting your way forward through what has befallen you and/or stepping up and offering a hand to and uplifting those who need help.

We Have and We Haven't

No one has experienced what is presently occurring in our communities and our businesses around the world. But adversity is not new, and many of us have been challenged in our lives and our businesses in all sorts of ways.

What has worked and has not worked in overcoming adversity and challenges is our reference point. And this reference point can provide an anchor and a pathway forward to those who may need it and those who are seeking to support others.

What follows comes from my formal learnings, personal experiences and through helping others. May it assist you in your journey forward.

Introduction

There are simple guiding principles that will anchor you in a position of stability and thereafter strengthen and enable you to plot the safest and most effective path forward. They are common sense, but that does not mean that in times of adversity that they will be to the forefront of your thinking, nor easy to sustain.

As the hole your business is falling into becomes more evident and deeper, and the chances of getting yourself out of it evaporate, you may become overwhelmed, depressed, unable to think clearly, desperate and possibly angry. You may lose hope.

None of these responses are unusual, and they should be expected but not accepted—as they will not help you in any way whatsoever to find solutions. They are a flight response and running away from the challenges facing your business is the last thing you want to do.

If you have been successful in your business then you know how to fight and fight well above your weight. This is the spirit of the entrepreneur, the person who seeded the original business idea, made it real, grew it to the success it has become. It is this spirit that you must find and leverage for all it can provide.

What is happening in this season is beyond anyone's planning and foresight. There is no shame and no blame, and you should not, in any way, allow such a sense to befall you. Hold your head high and prove your worth and character through how you accept loss and push your way forward.

Wake up each morning, take a deep breath, give thanks for the day that is about to commence, roll out of bed, both feet firmly planted on the ground and go into battle. Adopt this mantra of an approach and you will quickly find your energy is restored, actions and options emerging, and a future being built.

Here are the seven guiding principles that I believe will allow you to weather the storms and emerge stronger and more capable as a person. The greatest asset you have is you and it is *you* that we want to ensure is around to build an even greater business than whatever existed before.

Seven guiding principles:
1: Accept
2: Clarify
3: Action
4: Champions
5: Be Real
6: Care
7: A Light

What will be your daily mantra?
Write it here.

1. Accept

The first step you must take in moving forward through whatever challenges your business, and you, may be facing is acceptance. Acceptance is an honest and frank recognition of the challenges and a willingness to engage in finding that way forward actively. The elements of acceptance are:

✔ Accept and Adapt:

The disappearing customers and revenue are not within your control— the business of yesterday is no longer. Do not try to fight against it, adapt as best you can and evolve through and beyond it.

There is always a business for today and tomorrow. Businesses exist to meet the needs of customers. The present challenge is: What emerging needs can you adapt your business to meet?

✔ Release and Respond:

The quicker you release your images and paradigms of the business that did exist, the quicker you will be able to cut the losses and ignite a new future. But this will not happen while you firmly hold on to the past.

✔ Losses and More Losses:

There are and will be inevitable losses of wealth, assets, people, positions, relationships and more. Some you can save but there will be those beyond your influence and reach.

Identify what can be saved and what is most important for creating the new future—hold onto these as best you can. Allow all else to go and utilise what is left to your greatest advantage.

✔ Grieve and Permit:

What can you say about things that have taken a lifetime to build and then are gone, and you can do nothing about it?

Grieving will be present and real. Expect and acknowledge these feelings and permit them to exist. Do not express them through rage, anger, outbursts or blame. Do not feed them with alcohol, drugs or other forms of attempted suppression.

Allow them to be present and felt, and feel comfortable in recognising and saying that you are grieving over what might be the loss of years and even a lifetime's work.

✔ Truth and Connection:

Be open and truthful with everyone about what is happening in your business and life, and the fears that you are confronting. Don't hide them or lie about them, share openly, especially with partners, family and those closest to you. Do not allow even an ounce of pride to hold you back from this openness.

Everyone is impacted by what is happening in our world today, and your frankness may give them the strength to also share and seek support.

✔ Hand in Hand

There is a way forward, there is a future, and what has been lost is lost and belongs to yesterday. Acceptance is about that willingness to release the past and to step forward to create your new future. In doing so, be willing to accept the support of others and be even more willing to offer your hand in support to those whom you see and know need help.

Activate Acceptance

1. Accept

2. Release

3. Losses

4. Grieve

5. Truth

6. Together

2. Clarify

Clarity is about bringing to the table the facts and ideas that you need to consider so as to create actions. There are two parts to clarity: firstly, where you stand today and how that may track, and secondly, what options you can brainstorm for tomorrow.

Facts:

Bringing absolute clarity to your financial position and ensuring you know the financial standing of your business, you and others impacted is a must. This is not a time for 'thinking you knew' or 'what you understood to be the position'—it is the time for facts and full disclosure.

Seek whatever advice and support you will need to bring these facts, clarity and understanding to the table. It will take time, but it is a priority, and not something to be left for another day. If you do not undertake this task thoroughly you will probably find debts, non-compliance issues and legal actions chasing you for years to come and possibly impacting the new business you have built.

For some businesses, this will be an easier task than others depending on the nature of the business, its size and the complexity that taxation planning may have injected into your structures.

Here is a guide as to what you may need to gather and watch out for:

▶ Current period statements of financial position for each legal entity in your business group and also a statement of assets and liabilities for yourself, and possibly your spouse if they are 'exposed' to financial liability from the business.

▶ A corporate structure diagram that clearly reflects shareholdings leading up to the ultimate holding company and shareholders, allowing you to clearly see who owns what.

▶ Highlight and trace how the shareholding flows through the various entities and inter-company loans between legal entities as these may permit assets in one entity to be exposed to debt in other entities.

▶ Copies of all bank loan and other finance agreements and security documents and understand who the borrowers and guarantors are, what assets act as security and terms of and actions upon default.

▶ Copies of all lease, rental or any other financing agreements and understand who the borrowers and guarantors are, what assets act as security and terms of and actions upon default.

▶ A listing of all personal guarantees ever provided to banks, finance, lease or rental companies and suppliers that may remain current. Be careful as sometimes when you first start a business, you sign guarantees that are forgotten until a default occurs and you suddenly find yourself, your partner/spouse, parents and even friends are caught up in that default.

▶ With suppliers, be careful and check agreements and invoices for clauses that seek to withhold transfer of title in goods until payment is made in full. You may be holding stock that you think is yours, but you actually don't own it.

▶ In all forms of debt, finance etc. look for default provisions, who they may impact, assets at risk, how that flows through to other entities, what actions may possibly occur in default and understand what this all means. And then consider options for extension and/or relief under these agreements and in addition what further concessions and relief are currently being extended to support businesses in the current economic climate.

▶ Understand clearly and list out all outstanding obligations to employees and taxation authorities as you may become personally liable for these or face prosecution for non-compliance.

▶ Seek out information on the various support and relief packages that are presently being offered through various government agencies, banks and financial institutions.

The listing of items you need clarity around may be shorter or longer, but to move forward with confidence, you must nail this information and ensure all the 't's' are crossed and the 'i's' are dotted.

Clearly understand the financial position of your business group and those that it impacts and how any wind-up of that group will flow through the various entities and persons and how that impact may be lessened or mitigated, legally and fairly.

Where are you exposed, and how do you mitigate that exposure?

Ideas:

Brainstorm a list of ideas as to how you may lift the revenue in your business, what opportunities may exist where your business can pivot into new markets, emerging needs etc., and what resources and capabilities your business possess that may be leveraged into these new opportunities.

The people in your business are a critical resource and although paying wages with a declining revenue is a real and possibly unsustainable challenge, their contribution to your business's future is essential. Include them in the brainstorm and consider how their contribution may support your business, and at the same time, their continuing employment.

The following questions may assist in this process:

Openings:

▶ For your business, who are your customers, and what needs has your business been meeting?

▶ How are these needs changing, and what opportunities may this change provide?

▶ What key areas of need are arising in the community now?

▶ Are there any opportunities for your business to step in to meeting these emerging needs?

▶ What assets, resources and capabilities exist within your business that may be applied to needs that presently exist in the community?

Closings:

▶ Are there areas within your business that have never really performed to your expectation that you have not addressed? Should you take this opportunity to sell them off or close them down now?

▶ Are there surpluses or excesses in your business that can be released or cut back that will provide funds?

▶ What projects or activities can be curtailed?

▶ What can be sold?

▶ Which staff can you no longer support in employment—be careful as you will need these people when your business fires up again.

Deals:

▶ In addition to the areas of support that government, banks etc. are offering, where else can you possibly reduce the strain on your business? For example, landlords and suppliers. Can you negotiate reduced payments?

▶ Have you sat down with your workforce and discussed the current situation and how you may support each other to keep the business and their jobs afloat for today and importantly tomorrow?

▶ Are there any potential investors who are cashed up and interested in taking a longer-term view of your business who may be open to taking up equity? This could include suppliers.

▶ Are there any competitors that you may be able to merge with so the strength of two will allow both of you to sustain your businesses into the future?

▶ Does anything else come to mind?

Facts

Bring Clarity

Facts

Ideas

Ideas

3. Action

Acceptance and clarity will provide the foundations to plan for tomorrow—to plan to exit and close down what is necessary to survive and cut your losses, and to see what opportunities you can open for your business so that it may find new footings and grow into whatever shape or size may make sense.

The facts, as best as you can determine, should now be on the table, along with the options and possibilities that you see. Your focus is to cut the losses, retain resources and capabilities and set your sights and efforts on the future.

What are the non-negotiables, who and what can't you afford to lose if you are to start over? List them out and note why they are non-negotiable and place them in order of priority.

▶ Non-negotiables:

WHAT	WHY	PRIORITY

List on page 49

Pull the above together, get your head in the right place and list out your actions. What are you going to do?

These categories of actions may assist you:

▶ Financial risks to be mitigated:

_____

_____

_____

_____

_____

_____

▶ Government support to be sought:

_____

_____

_____

_____

_____

_____

_____

▶ Concessions from banks, financiers etc.:

_____

_____

_____

_____

_____

_____

▶ Rebates, reductions etc. from landlords and suppliers:

_____

_____

_____

_____

_____

_____

▶ Partnering with employees:

_____

_____

_____

_____
_____
_____
_____

▶ What to sell:

_____
_____
_____
_____
_____
_____
_____

▶ What to reduce:

_____
_____
_____
_____
_____
_____
_____
_____

▶ What to close:

_____

_____

_____

_____

_____

_____

_____

▶ New products, services and markets to enter:

_____

_____

_____

_____

_____

_____

▶ Who may be able to help me:

_____

_____

_____

▶ Whom to let go:

▶ What else:

Your game plan will likely include:

- ✔ plug the holes
- ✔ cut the losses
- ✔ defer payments
- ✔ seek relief
- ✔ retain capability
- ✔ cash up where possible
- ✔ find new opportunities now
- ✔ drive revenue, and
- ✔ look for support.

Put into action your game plan, make all of this happen and continually refer to and update your plan as everything around you evolves.

My Game Plan

List Non-Negotiables

My Game Plan

Plug, Cut, Defer, Seek, Retain, Cash, Find, Drive, Look.

My Game Plan

Plug, Cut, Defer, Seek, Retain, Cash, Find, Drive, Look.

4. Champions

Strength through unity and humility should be your mantra. Do not try to undertake the journey of closing down all or parts of your business and then restarting by yourself.

Don't be foolish nor prideful, reach out to others for support and offer to help those who you see and know are struggling. There is a strength when people come together in support of each other—leverage that strength.

Your Champions:

Identify three people whom you know will gladly 'have your back', support you to their utmost and importantly be honest brokers in the advice and opinions that you will seek from them. This will be your inner circle who will champion you through the challenges you are facing and stick with you until all is achieved and then some.

They may well not be the people whom you have surrounded yourself with to date, and therefore do not turn to your default setting without a pause and careful consideration.

Be very careful about inviting anyone to be your champion who is or has:

▶ A financial interest in your business such as a business partner or investor, and possibly even some of your current advisors. Engage with them, seek their advice but keep them at arms-length unless you know through experience where their heart lies and that they will not place their interests ahead of yours. Spouses are exempt from this exclusion.

▶ More interested in themselves than helping others—pride, ego, selfishness.

▶ Full of doom and gloom and can only see the downside and all the things that you have done wrong in life and business.

▶ No real interest in you or your business but will come along if there is a dollar in it for them.

You should be seeking a mix of people who:

▶ Have a heart for you and your welfare.

▶ Know you well and over an extended period of time.

▶ Have a good business mind.

▶ Want to see you succeed.

▶ You trust without hesitation.

▶ Will be honest and frank with you.

▶ Are of integrity.

Not any one person may have all of these traits, but as your team of champions, they will cover all these bases.

Make a list of persons, rank them in your order of preference, and ask them if they are willing to come alongside you and support you as a person in journeying forward through the challenges you are facing and will face.

These are my Champions:

NAME	MOBILE	EMAIL

List on page 60

And I have committed to meet with them on:

Every _____ at _____ am/pm

And we will meet at

_____

_____

_____

_____

Their Role:

The role of your champions is to support you and your role is to allow them to do this. This is where humility plays such an important part.

Humility is simply the willingness to listen to others, to be open and vulnerable, and take on board their advice. If you cannot bring yourself to be humble then your champions will be wasting their time, and you also, as your ego and pride will prevent you from truly hearing what they are saying.

In all decisions that you are about to make, seek confirmation from your champions. You may speak to your business partners, professional advisors, etc., but your champions are your inner circle who have your back.

When you have developed your action list from '3' above, present it to your champions and allow them to speak into the actions you are about to take. Listen very carefully to what they say, question them on their views/advice, and reflect carefully if not in agreement.

Your champions are also present to uplift you, inject you with vigour and to make sure you personally do not fall into a hole from which you do not or cannot emerge. To allow them to do this, meet with them regularly at set times and do not defer these meetings. You don't have to meet them all at the same time, every time; it's probably better not to as your relationship with each will likely be different.

But it is also good that your champions come together as a team and meet with you as a team. When presenting action items or considering business decisions is a good time to introduce this formality. This allows your champions to connect with each other, share ideas and thoughts, worries and concerns. It allows them to function as a team.

So, who's on your team? Ring them and meet with them now. And who could you possibly be a champion for?

These are the three people that I can offer to be a champion for:

1: _____

_____

2: _____

_____

3: _____

_____

My Champions

List of Possible Champions

My Champions

List of Confirmed Champions

5. Be Real

Be authentic to who you are as a business leader and what your business stands for. Please do not abandon your principles and values in the face of adversity but allow them to be your strength.

As all appears to be lost, as you find yourself overwhelmed and just incapable of knowing what to do, you can find yourself abandoning what has been your values and principles in an attempt merely to survive. Or should I say, what you think will be survival at that time, but as you look back, you may well regret your actions. Do not allow yourself to fall into this trap.

Your champions exist to hold you true and honest to who they know you are. But you also must be clear on the values and principles that underpin and define who you are as a person.

If you have never taken the time to reflect on what defines you as a person, then take some time out and reflect on this now. Do not allow the adversity of today to catch you off guard and push you down a path which is simply not you.

I'm not sure if many people have reflected on what their purpose is for their life, or what virtues/values they seek to anchor their lives in. There are processes that you can use to support you in discovering these attributes and strengths which can be quite defining in your life. This is probably not a journey for you to undertake with the current challenges but certainly something to put on your to-do list.

For today, just take a few minutes and list out what attributes you would like to see in yourself. Once you have this list, discuss it with your champions and then refine and settle the list. This will now serve as an anchor, a benchmark if you like, and all actions and decisions should be confirmed against this list.

If it may help, here is my life purpose and values that I seek to follow in all that I do:

'My purpose is to enable others to bring success to their lives. And in following this path, I seek courage, determination, humility and love.'

So, as an example as to how purpose and values act as an anchor:

▶ If I was to axe all my employees without considering their welfare or how I may retain them, would l be living up to these attributes?—I would say no.

▶ If I gave up all hope for my future as a businessperson?—Again no.

▶ What about if I was to take advantage of others?—Again no.

▶ What about if I step up to the challenge, engage with others to seek their support and find solutions, if I was taking new risks to build a business that can survive and then thrive?—I would say yes, I am living the attributes I aspire to.

Knowing whom I seek to be and the attributes I aspire to allows me to be authentic, to be real and to build my life on and against this foundation.

Who are you as a person? What do you aspire to be known for as a person? And how would that person step forward in the current adversities? Now list the attributes that describe you and live your life by them.

Who Am I?

How would you describe yourself. Jot down a few points.

Who Am I?

Possibilities.

List out those traits and attributes that you believe define you as a person. Discuss these with your Champions and see if they agree.

Who Am I?

Confirmed.

List out those values and virtues that have been agreed to by your Champions and you.

6. Care

The core strength of your business rests in you as an individual and the energies and ideas you can bring to your business.

You must 'care' for yourself as a priority. If you are unable to sustain and strengthen your physical, emotional and mental condition and resilience, all your efforts will fall short of what is possible.

Substances in any form are not a substitute for good health; however, I personally exempt coffee and chocolate from this list—but I try to take them in moderation.

So, what does care look like? Here's a list:

▶ Acceptance—grieving and moving forward with the support of your champions.

▶ Breathing well in times of stress—pausing and breathing slowly and deeply through your nose and preferably out through your nose, with the exhalation being longer than the inhalation.

▶ Stretching and opening your body—creates space and allows energy to flow and stress to be released.

▶ Sit upright quietly, close your eyes gently and meditate—twice a day, morning and evening, for at least 15 minutes and just allow all the thoughts buzzing around in your head to buzz, observe them, release them, focus on your breath, relax and sink into the quiet.

▶ Have your action plan to hand—write it up and carry it with you always and when moments of doubt arise, pull it out, look at it and reassure yourself that you have a plan and move on.

▶ Exercise—in some form for 30 minutes every day, just walking can be great. I am not a fan of pushing yourself to your limit and exhaustion. To me, this increases the stress on your body and nervous system at a time when you should be giving yourself a bit more space for rest and recovery. Exercise but don't overdo it.

▶ Drink lots of water—throughout the day and sustain really good hydration. Note: water, no substitutes.

▶ Connect and talk—don't go into

isolation, have someone whom you can talk to close by and speak to them openly and honestly, and ask them just to 'really listen'. This is a great release, and if you are fortunate enough to own a dog, they really listen well but they are no substitute for human listening.

▶ Hugs—if at all possible, find someone who is happy to give you lots of hugs every day; no not sex just hugs.

▶ Eat well and regularly—eat well every day but don't over-eat and keep the rushed meals and junk food to an absolute minimum. Don't work and eat, rather pause and eat quietly.

▶ Sleep early, wake early—form clear habits around sleeping and waking at the same time every day. You are in training to save your business, support that effort with great rest.

▶ End of day—establish a habit around the close of work for the day. Don't allow work to permeate every moment of every day in actions or thought. Your mind needs time to turn off to rejuvenate, and this then permits innovation and creativity to flourish.

▶ Be thankful—for what you have
and give thanks each morning for the
opportunities that the day will present.
You will be surprised how an 'attitude
of gratitude' opens up opportunities
throughout a day.

▶ Family—keep family close, be honest
and open with them, and never allow
anger or frustration to enter those
relationships. Discipline yourself so
these emotions never come home
with you.

▶ Faith—if you are a person of faith
then turn into that faith and find the
peace that it will offer.

Care is about being kind to yourself, not
as a form of weakness but as a discipline,
as you recognise being kind is founded
in strength, and strength in yourself
is what is most important in times of
adversity.

And importantly, being kind to yourself
opens the doors for you to be kind
to others and support them on their
challenging journey as well.

Attitude

Acceptance - Action plan - End of Day - Thankful

Core Strength

Openness
Breathing - Stretching - Exercise

Peace
Meditate - Connect - Family - Faith

Core Strength

Energy
Hydrate - Hugs - Eat - Sleep

7. A Light

Always seek, find and hold onto the light in your life, business and work. That light represents hope and joy and allows you to overcome any adversity that may try to match and defeat you.

When you are up against it, and you are literally losing everything you have worked for (and love) and can't see the opening, it can become very dark, very quickly. And in that darkness, there can only be loss. Never allow that darkness to settle upon and overwhelm you, nor such to happen to someone for whom you are a champion.

Shine the light into your and their lives.

If you have never experienced the loss of a lifetime's work—the identity, purpose and connection that goes with it—then it might be hard to imagine the how or why and to what extent it can impact someone. And literally, the fight of a lifetime they have on their hands. But accept that such grieving and loss can quickly overwhelm someone even though they may, from a distance, seem okay.

With what is occurring in businesses around the world today, and to their owners and others connected with them, there is a real and present risk to life and prolonged mental and emotional suffering.

Hope must be seeded and maintained for the light to be present. In your life, and in that of others, do not allow that light to be extinguished or lost. Follow the guiding principles set out in the preceding pages, and the light will be present.

For those around you, look deeply into their eyes, care for them and be their light until they are able to spark it in theirs.

Hope and joy should be ever-present in everyone's life. We can sometimes struggle with the adversities that life throws at us and the losses it expects us to take, but within us all is that hope, that joy and that light.

In times of adversity, dig deeper, anchor yourself in that light and make it who you are: a person who walks through adversity and comes out the other side smiling and better off, with an attitude of thanks for the lessons that life has just allowed you to learn. Use those lessons to make your life and that of others even better than before.

Bring it on and watch me show you how the right attitude to life makes any adversity just like a pleasant afternoon breeze.

So, what is light? Light is your reason for living and striving forward every day. Light can come in many forms. Some would say it is family or a partner. For others it can be faith or a specific goal or a vision. And many times, it is a stubbornness that says, 'I am not going to be defeated, I will win!'

Make sure you identify the light in your life and keep it strong and bright.

My Light—My Life

What has been your joy and motivation in life?

Possibilities

What do you think may bring you joy in the future?
List and discuss with your Champions.

Confirmed

Write a brief paragraph on where your joy, your light, will be found as you journey forward.

Your Journey

Be very clear with yourself, there is a journey that you are about to embark on as you confront the business challenges that this season is presenting.

You will need to fight and draw upon all your resources and strength in this journey as you travel forward to find a solid landing and foundation for your business—a landing upon which you can rebuild your business.

This journey requires preparation, planning and focused execution to be successful. You cannot allow yourself to become weakened on this journey or you will be in even greater jeopardy.

The principles that will guide you are as follows:

▶ Accept the realities of the losses that have and will befall you, release this past and engage actively in creating a new future.

88 | Going Broke Staying Sane

▶ Bring clarity to your financial position, know your losses and risks, mitigate them, and craft a path forward through this adversity. Go forward from a position of knowledge, not doubt.

▶ Create your action plan and execute it with a determination you have not mustered before while always adapting to emerging challenges and evolving opportunities.

▶ Draw your team of three champions to your side and leverage that combined strength.

▶ Do not allow adversity to overwhelm those traits and values that define who you are as a person.

▶ Establish the care programme that will underpin and sustain your personal strength and wellbeing, and make it a non-negotiable deliverable.

▶ Always see the light in your life and hold onto it with both hands as it is your life vest at the most challenging of times.

▶ Reach out and help others in distress and find the strength that comes through helping others.

And through these principles journey forward through adversity and succeed.

This is your journey, start now and don't stop until you reach the safe landing on the other side.

What will be your first step?

Active Knowledge®
Daily Mentor Series

The journey to enduring success does not stop
at the last page of this book.

It is a daily endeavour in which each day you take a small
step forward building on the previous day. And your
strength and success will compound day after day.

You are not on this journey alone—I am here
to support you.

The QR code below will allow you to subscribe,
free of charge, to my Daily Mentor Series which will
deliver into your Inbox, each day for the next 90 days,
an Active Knowledge® quote tailored to guide
and support you on your journey.

Active Knowledge® quotes are one-part thinking and one-part doing. They deliver knowledge that drives action and wisdom that inspires momentum. They will become a critical resource.

All the best on your journey forward.

Richard Shrapnel PhD

BUSINESS STRATEGIST

About Richard

Richard Shrapnel has a passion for growing exceptional businesses and has spent his life understanding what makes some businesses great and others just ordinary. He understands strategy, growth, and competitiveness. He knows the theory and the practice, how to craft it and, more importantly, how to deliver it. As a strategist, his focus is on what creates success and understanding not only what makes businesses successful but also the people behind them. He is a writer, speaker, and advisor and he supports business leaders around the world build great businesses of all shapes and sizes.

The Initials After My Name
▶ PhD in Business Strategy—Australian Graduate School of Entrepreneurship, Swinburne University of Technology, Melbourne, Australia.

▶ Master of Business in Organisational Competitiveness (by research)—Monash University, Melbourne, Australia.

▶ Bachelor of Business (Accountancy)—Caulfield Institute of Technology, Melbourne, Australia.

▶ Fellow of the Institute of Managers and Leaders (FIML).

▶ Fellow of the Strategic Planning Society.

▶ Member of the Institute of Chartered Accountants of Australia.

▶ Member of the Strategic Management Society.

▶ Graduate Australian Institute of Company Directors (International Directors).

▶ Certified N.E.W.S Coach.

▶ Certified Lego Serious Play Facilitator.

richardshrapnel.com
 drrichardshrapnel

Reimagining My Self-Image
(read pages 9-10)

Write a few words that describes the new future you are
about to create and what it will mean to you.
Carry this image of your future with you and make it real.